Ode:
Salute to the New York School 1950–1970
(A Libretto)

Ode : Salute to the New York School

1950–1970

LETTER MACHINE EDITIONS TUCSON AZ DENVER CO

Peter Gizzi

(A Libretto)

Published by Letter Machine Editions
Tucson, Arizona 85721
lettermachine.org

Design and Composition by Michael Labenz

Printed in Canada

Cataloging-in-Publication Data is on file at the Library of Congress.
ISBN-13: 978-0-9815-2277-7

Distributed to the trade by Small Press Distribution *(spdbooks.org)*

Cover Image: detail of *Untitled (downtown),* mixed media collage
Photo credit: Stephen Petegorsky

for Clark Coolidge

down town

Contents

Cento

A car roars over a conversation

Ah! such scissors of wind we are tearing our validity

A little horse trots up with a letter in its mouth, which is
read with eagerness as we gallop into the flame

All revolutions have betrayed themselves by slush of
feeling

A man signs a shovel and so he digs

And the nerve-ends evolved to cope with instant danger
do not know what to tell the brain so they think about it

As if nobody believes what anybody tells them, gray in
the cafe and the shiny rain

A sigh loaded with stale revolt like a freshwater tear

Bloom, flare, blink open

Born eaves clump bounce

But do we really need anything more to be sorry about

But Ned is lazy, the monkey has to do it all

By day I sleep, an obscurantist, lost in dreams of lists

Depersonalized angels refer you to nothing and you are
nothing, meat stencils

Did you ever read the wet page of the earth?

File prayer tines

Fond memories of childhood, and the pleasant orange trolleys

For the first time in many years Kafka's mother enters the
room to kiss him good-night

Gladly smothered in windows

Glee a short road across my face

Goodbye, Father! Goodbye, pupils. Goodbye, my master and
my dame

Ha ha ha

Have I worn out my distracting powers to doze witless
    into the scape of night, empty of detail and excuse

He has banged into your wall of air, your hubris

His substance utters a sun above the stoves of our discourse

History, what did the Rose do?

How many ways to die for a window

I am interested in "reading" and in controlling reading speed

I am whizzed, suspended perpetually around the same
    green corner, spurious alb!

"I am your pineapple sunrise! I am your vanilla wristwatch!
    I am your whip!" says the Boy Scout.

I bit my lip as he scraped my semen off the floor

I'd give a bunch of bananas for a sniff of your behind, oh yes!

I'd like to buy a house for your mind, white curtains

If Joan says I'm wounded, then I'm wounded

If things are the way we say they are then why do we say
they are

I got to catch a bus for Altoona where I can smile again

I have won myself over to this cause. I am yours! You are
mine! Light bulb! Holy Ghost!

I'll trade one red sucker for two blue ones

I look at the Himalayas; they neither sit nor stand

I love you like a sheriff searches for a walnut

In a church's tiered and April-green alcoves

In the bat light, in the bugger Darkness

In the murdersome chorus lines of the snow an entire
bird fell biffing from off a tire

In you, I feel the new kite. What are your feelings like?

In Y's and V's and W's an elm ascends smoothly as an
Otis Elevator

I prefer "you" in the plural, I want "you"

I remember jerking off to sexual fantasies involving John
Kerr. And Montgomery Clift

I salute that various field

Is it dirty, does it look dirty, that's what you think of in the city

I speak as a wife to the capsizing

I stagered from the car nut reall hurt jus shok op

I think that's enough sex for today, d-d-d-don't you?

It is a distinct pleasure, and a marble-shaped pain, to be
caught while walking out in the rain

It's me (was) & now it's you

It's not that I'm curious. On the contrary, I am bored but it's
my duty to be attentive, I am needed by things

It's so clean you could flush ten million toilets into it and it
would stay the same

It's so original, hydrogenic, anthropomorphic, fiscal, post-
anti-esthetic, bland, unpicturesque and William Carlos
Williamsian!

"It was Saturday night and I just got toed"

I waken, read, write long letters and wander restlessly when
leaves are blowing

I want to walk around in you breezily, o world, when I'm
young

Left behind in New York City, & oof!

Let's warm up the simian pianola

Like watching wind push seaflowers straight across your
eyelids

Love makes it poetic though blue

Many stars are in the sky, I asked Mother to help me,
afterward

May's favorite game is *fan tan.* She always wins the antes
by gooping herself up with man tan, after she takes
off her scanties

My Army likes you so much loves you I think so much
they are marching to your hit recording *Me!*

My flesh abides

My heart is blue and my foot has been ruined by the night

My love is a lurking toy

Naked arms, his chief activity, provided an annex of joy
and compact tours

Near Paris, there is a boat. Near this boat live the beautiful
Woods

Night again again

Not the shadow you leave behind but the opening ahead

No turning back, no rewrite, no voice! in this poem, now,
not to look nor creep back to the stark horror

Now as my questioning but admiring gaze expands to
magnificent outposts

O blue tapeworm, sonnet of powerful indifference, nest

One of them said, "Ha ha! your spectacles are broken"

Open the mind of the paralytic stooge for seamy madness to
discover a call

Our habits ask us for instructions

Oxygen

Parachutes, my love, could carry us higher than this mid- air
in which we tremble

Rainbows. Many tomorrows. My name is Tom

Really, I thought that fish could cry

Rose bud, I love your pout, love the ash-built slope

Saviors of connections and spit, dial HYacinth 9-9945, "Isn't
that a conundrum?"

Six knobs, four in heaven, makes ten

Snow White had brought the music back

Swig Pepsi & drape the bent frame in something "blue for
going out"

That's not a cross look it's a sign of life

The black eyes ruffled the field of expectant spirits smooth on ice

The fate of the fake nostalgia of beebees lost under the
furniture hulks

The grin of sleep is in the wind

The handkerchiefs as guards, the interjections orphaned

Their eyes grow louche at the exact second they start their slide

The last party to be seized at twilight, and time was cold to
the lovers

The mind reaches forward gets hooked on the horizon and
just hangs there

The next day a verb drove up, and created the sentence

The pony-spoor of hotblood bank chip, far away from in
outsize day

The quiet evening street, I spend a week in my underwear
reading Williams and drinking orange soda, both in
California

The radiator came on & the geraniums died

There is nothing worse than elephant love

There is, with each soft clang, a marble fist

These   ing   those

The tone is hard is heard is the coming of strength out of
    night: unfeared

The tonic resonance of pill when used as in "she is a pill"

The train comes bearing joy; the sparks it strikes
    illuminate the table

The tremendous reassurance of being at the dinner table
    and tense, a stalwart melody

They are preparing to begin again: problems, new pennant
    up the flagpole in a predicated romance

This honey is delicious but it burns the throat

Truth is truth on an empty street at noon

Twelve Bells! Benny's on the ropes! Twelve Bells! He has
    no feet! Twelve Bells! He can't make gloves!

Up north in the Aurora Borealis the blame falls like rain

We live in our own hip pocket, nodding out to rush back in

What obsolete! what lift! geronimo of confusion

When Andrew's letter arrived, three agents had already gone
in vain to search for Dog Boss

When the cows and the leaves begin to fall, they fall like
falsehood

When we join them we will show them trophies of old smoke

Where green changes itself into LIFE

Whose impetus is irresistible: Get out of here!

Who will smile, & love you, at your leisure

Will they search for rust among the fake doubloons?

Yet the cars do not cheat, even their colors perform in storm

You can feel the wind in the room, the curtains are moving in
the draft and a door slowly closes

You select something small like a pimple and quick as a
wink that's all there is

You think of your art which has become important like a
plow on the flat land.

Bibliography

THREE
DIMENSION
COMICS

1950

1951

1952

O'Hara, Frank. *A City Winter.* New York: Tibor de Nagy Editions.

Love makes it poetic though blue

1953

Ashbery, John. *Turandot*. New York: Tibor de Nagy Editions.

~~But~~ open the mind of the paralytic stooge for seamy madness to discover a call.

Koch, Kenneth. *Poems*. New York: Tibor de Nagy Editions.

I love you like a sheriff searches for a walnut.

O'Hara, Frank. *Oranges.* New York: Tibor de Nagy Editions.

I have won myself over to this cause. I am yours! You are mine! Light bulb! Holy Ghost!

1954

1955

1956

Ashbery, John. *Some Trees.* New Haven: Yale University Press.
The train comes bearing joy; the sparks it strikes illuminate the table.

Denby, Edwin. *Mediterrianian Cities.* New York: Wittenborn.
In a church's tiered and April-green alcoves.

1957

O'Hara, Frank. *Meditations in an Emergency.* New York: Grove Press.
It's not that I'm curious. On the contrary, I am bored / but it's my duty to be attentive, I am needed by things.

1958

1959

Berrigan, Ted. *A Lily for My Love.* Providence: Privately published.
(not available)

Koch, Kenneth. *Ko, Or a Season on Earth.* New York: Grove Press.
When Andrew's letter / Arrived, three agents had already gone / In vain to search for Dog Boss.

1960

Ashbery, John. *The Poems.* New York: Tiber Press.
this honey is delicious but it burns the throat

Guest, Barbara. *The Location of Things.* New York: Tibor de Nagy Editions.

Parachutes, my love, could carry us higher / than this mid-air in which we tremble

Koch, Kenneth. *Permanently.* New York: Tiber Press.

The next day a verb drove up, and created the sentence

O'Hara, Frank. *Odes.* New York: Tiber Press.

but do we really need anything more to be sorry about

O'Hara, Frank. *Second Avenue.* New York: Totem/Corinth Press.

Saviors of connections and spit, dial HYacinth 9-9945, "Isn't that / a conundrum?"

Padgett, Ron. *Summer Balloons.* Tulsa: Privately published.

my love is a lurking toy

Schuyler, James. *Salute.* New York: Tiber Press.

I salute that various field.

1961

Berkson, Bill. *Saturday Night Poems.* New York: Tibor de Nagy Editions.

All revolutions have betrayed themselves / by slush of feeling

Elmslie, Kenward. *Pavilions.* New York: Tibor de Nagy Editions.

My Army likes you so much loves you I think so much they are marching to your hit recording Me!

1962

Ashbery, John. *The Tennis Court Oath.* Middletown: Wesleyan University Press.

A little horse trots up with a letter in its mouth, which is read with eagerness as we gallop into the flame.

Guest, Barbara. *Poems: The Location of Things; Archaics; The Open Skies.* New York: Doubleday.

You think of your art / which has become important / like a plow / on the flat land

Koch, Kenneth. *Thank You and Other Poems.* New York: Grove Press.

Fond memories of childhood, and the pleasant orange trolleys

1963

Denby, Edwin. *"C" Magazine.* Vol 1, No. 4, Special Edwin Denby Issue. New York: September.

Rose bud, I love your pout, love the ash-built slope.

Sanders, Ed. *Poems from Jail.* San Francisco: City Lights.

My flesh abides

1964

Berrigan, Ted. *The Sonnets.* New York: Lorenz and Ellen Gude.

A man / signs a shovel and so he digs.

Lima, Frank. *Inventory.* New York: Tibor de Nagy Editions.

Twelve Bells / Benny's on the ropes / Twelve Bells / He has no feet / Twelve Bells / He can't make gloves

O'Hara, Frank. *Audit Magazine.* Vol. 4, No. 1, Frank O'Hara Issue. Buffalo.

It's so original, hydrogenic, anthropomorphic, fiscal, post-anti-esthetic, bland, unpicturesque and William Carlos Williamsian!

O'Hara, Frank. *Lunch Poems.* San Francisco: City Lights.

Is it dirty / does it look dirty / that's what you think of in the city.

Padgett, Ron. *In Advance of a Broken Arm.* New York: C Press.

~~But now there is~~ the tremendous reassurance of being / At the dinner table and tense, a stalwart melody

Sanders, Ed. *King Lord/Queen Freak.* Cleveland: Renegade Press.

In the / bat light / in the bugger / Darkness

Sanders, Ed. *The Toe Queen Poems.* New York: Fuck You Press.

"It was Saturday night and I just got toed"

Veitch, Tom. *Literary Days.* New York: C Press.

I bit my lip as he scraped my semen off the floor

1965

Berrigan, Ted. *Living with Chris.* New York: Boke Press.

There is nothing worse than elephant love.

Ceravolo, Joe. *Fits of Dawn.* New York: C Press.

What obsolete! what lift! / geronimo of confusion

Gallup, Dick. *Hinges.* New York: C Press.
Will they search for rust / among the fake doubloons?

Greenwald, Ted. *Lapstrake.* New York: Lines Press.
The black eyes ruffled the field / of expectant spirits smooth on ice

MacAdams, Lewis. *City Money.* Oxford Burning Water Press.
I got to catch a bus for Altoona where I can smile again.

O'Hara, Frank. *Love Poems (Tentative Title).* New York: Tibor de Nagy Editions.
That's not a cross look it's a sign of life

Padgett, Ron. *In Advance of a Broken Arm.* 2nd edition. New York: C Press.
Let's warm up the simian pianola.

Sanders, Ed. *Peace Eye.* Cleveland: Frontier Press.
No turning back / no rewrite / no voice! / in this poem, now, not to look / nor creep back to the stark horror.

Shapiro, David. *January.* New York: Holt, Rinehart and Winston.
Really, I thought that fish could cry.

1966

Acconci, Vito [and E. Lagomarsino]. *Double Bubble.* New York: Privately published.
The handkerchiefs as guards, the interjections orphaned

Ashbery, John. *Rivers and Mountains.* New York: Holt, Rinehart and Winston.

I prefer "you" in the plural, I want "you."

Berrigan, Ted. *The Sonnets.* 2nd edition. New York: Grove Press.

I waken, read, write long letters and / wander restlessly when leaves are blowing.

Brodey, Jim. *Fleeing Madly South.* New York: Clothsline Editions.

the quiet evening street / I spend a week in my underwear / reading Williams / and drinking orange soda / both in California.

Carroll, Jim. *Organic Trains.* New York: Penny Press.

Ah! such scissors of wind / we are tearing our validity

Clark, Tom. *Airplanes.* Essex: Once Press.

I'd give a bunch of bananas for a sniff of your behind, oh yes!

Clark, Tom. *The Sand Burg.* London: Ferry Press.

Rainbows. Many tomorrows. My name is Tom.

Coolidge, Clark. *Flag Flutter & U. S. Electric.* New York: Lines Press.

The fate of the fake nostalgia of beebees lost under the furniture hulks.

Kolmar, Richard. *Games.* New York: Lines Press.

There is, with each soft clang, a marble fist

Padgett, Ron. *Sky.* London: Goliard Press.

It's so clean you could flush ten million toilets into it and it would stay the same.

Padgett, Ron. *Tone Arm.* Essex: Once Press.

you select something small like a pimple / and quick as a wink that's all there is

Perreault, John. *Camouflage.* New York: Lines Press.

"I am your pineapple sunrise! I am your vanilla wristwatch! I am your whip!" says the Boy Scout.

Schuyler, James. *May 24th or So.* New York: Tibor de Nagy Editions.

In Y's and V's and W's an elm ascends smoothly as an Otis Elevator.

Veitch, Tom. *Toad Poems.* Essex, Once Press.

It is a distinct pleasure / And a marble-shaped pain / To be caught while walking / Out in the rain.

1967

Ashbery, John. *Selected Poems.* London: Jonathan Cape.

I'll trade one red sucker for two blue ones.

Berrigan, Ted and Ron Padgett. *Bean Spasms.* New York: Kulchur Press.

Ha ha ha

Berrigan, Ted. *Many Happy Returns.* New York: Angel Hair. (single sheet)

Swig Pepsi & drape the bent frame in something "blue for going out"

Brodey, Jim. *Identikit.* New York: Angel Hair.

The pony-spoor of hotblood bank chip, far away from in outsize day.

Brownstein, Michael. *Behind the Wheel.* New York: C Press.

Truth is truth on an empty street at noon

Ceravolo, Joe. *Wild Flowers Out of Gas.* New York: Tibor de Nagy Editions.

I speak as a wife to the capsizing

Clark, Tom. *The Emperor of the Animals.* London: Goliard Press.

His substance utters a sun above the stoves of our discourse

Coolidge, Clark. *Clark Coolidge.* New York: Lines Press.

born eaves clump bounce

Elmslie, Kenward [Joe Brainard, illus]. *The 1967 Game Calender.* New York: Privately Published.

May's favorite game is fan tan. *She always wins the antes / By gooping herself up with man tan, / after she takes off her scanties.*

Elmslie, Kenward. *Power Plant Poems.* New York: C Press.

When we join them / we will show them trophies of old smoke

O'Hara, Frank. *Meditations in an Emergency. 2nd edition.* New York: Grove Press.

He has banged into your wall / of air, your hubris

Padgett, Ron and Ted Berrigan. *Bean Spasms.* New York: Kulchur Press.

Ha ha ha

Padgett, Ron. *100,000 Fleeing Hilda.* New York: Boke Press.

many stars are in the sky / I asked Mother to help me / afterward

Sanders, Ed. *Peace Eye (Enlarged edition).* Cleveland: Frontier Press.
bloom, flare, blink open

Saroyan, Aram. *Coffee Coffee.* New York: 0 to 9.
oxygen

Torregian, Sotere. *The Golden Palomino Bites the Clock.* New York: Angel Hair.
I am whizzed, suspended perpetually around the same / Green corner / Spurious alb!

Warsh, Lewis. *The Suicide Rates.* Eugene, Oregon: Toad Press.
How many ways to die for a window

1968

Ashbery, John. *Sunrise in Suburbia.* New York: The Phoenix Book Shop.
The tone is hard is heard / Is the coming of strength out of night: unfeared.

Ashbery, John. *Three Madrigals.* New York: Poets Press.
The last party to be seized / at twilight, and time was cold / to the lovers.

Brodey, Jim. *Long Distance Quote.* Los Angeles: Mustard Seed Press. (broadside)
my heart is blue / and my foot / has been ruined by the / night

Carey, Steve. *Smith Going Backward.* San Francisco: Cranium Press.
Gladly smothered in windows

Ceravolo, Joe. *Spring in This World of Poor Mutts.* New York: Columbia University Press / Frank O'Hara Foundation.

In you, I feel / the new kite. / What are your feelings / like?

Clark, Tom (with Ron Padgett). *Bun.* New York: Angel Hair.

I'd like to buy a house for your mind / white curtains

Coolidge, Clark. *ING.* New York: Angel Hair.

these / ing / those

Elmslie, Kenward. *The Champ.* Los Angeles: Black Sparrow Press.

Naked arms, his chief activity, / provided an annex of joy and compact tours.

Fagin, Larry. *Parade of the Caterpillars.* New York: Angel Hair.

The radiator came on & the geraniums died.

Guest, Barbara. *The Blue Stairs.* New York: Corinth Books.

Yet the cars / do not cheat, even their colors perform in storm.

Koch, Kenneth. *Poems from 1952 and 1953.* Los Angeles: Black Sparrow.

In the murdersome chorus lines of the snow / An entire bird fell biffing from off a tire.

Mayer, Bernadette. *Story.* New York: 0 To 9.

History / what did the Rose do?

Saroyan, Aram. *Aram Saroyan.* New York: Random House.

night / again / again

Schjeldahl, Peter. *White Country.* New York: Corinth Books.
As if nobody believes what anybody tells them / Gray in the cafe and the shiny rain

Towle, Tony. *After Dinner We Take a Drive into the Night.* New York: Tibor de Nagy.
and the nerve-ends evolved to cope with instant danger / do not know what to tell the brain so they think about it

Waldman, Anne. *On the Wing.* New York: Boke Press.
The mind reaches forward / gets hooked on the horizon / and just hangs there

Warsh, Lewis. *Hijacking.* New York: Boke Press.
A sigh loaded with stale revolt / Like a freshwater tear

1969

Ashbery, John. *Fragment.* Los Angeles: Black Sparrow Press.
Our habits ask us for instructions.

Berkson, Bill [Joe Brainard, illus]. *Life Begins at Zero.* New York: Privately Published.
I think that's enough sex for today, d-d-d-don't you?.

Berkson, Bill. *Shining Leaves.* New York: Angel Hair Books.
Six knobs, / four in heaven, / makes ten.

Berrigan, Ted. *A Fragment.* London: Cape Goliard Press. (broadside)
Left behind in New York City, & oof!

Berrigan, Ted. *Many Happy Returns.* New York: Corinth Books.

By day I sleep, an obscurantist, lost in dreams of lists.

Berrigan, Ted. *Peace.* Detroit: Alternative Press. (broadside)

who will smile, & love you, at your leisure

Brownstein, Michael. *Highway to the Sky.* New York: Columbia University Press / Frank O'Hara Foundation.

Glee a short road across my face.

Clark, Tom. *Stones.* New York: Harper & Row.

One of them said, "Ha ha! your spectacles are broken."

Elmslie, Kenward. *Album.* New York: Kulchur Press.

Their eyes grow louche at the exact second they start their slide

Koch, Kenneth. *The Pleasures of Peace and Other Poems.* New York: Grove Press.

Snow White had brought the music back.

Koch, Kenneth. *When the Sun Tries to Go On.* Los Angeles: Black Sparrow.

O blue tapeworm, sonnet of powerful indifference, nest

O'Hara, Frank. *Odes.* 2nd edition. New York: Poets Press.

If Joan says I'm wounded, then I'm wounded

O'Hara, Frank. *Two Pieces.* London: Long Hair Books.

~~that~~ up north in the Aurora Borealis / the blame falls like rain.

Padgett, Ron. *Great Balls of Fire.* New York: Holt, Rinehart and Winston.

When the cows and the leaves begin to fall / They fall like falsehood

Perreault, John. *Luck.* New York: Kulchur Press.

I am interested in "reading" and in controlling reading speed.

Saroyan, Aram. *Pages.* New York: Random House.

a car roars over a / conversation

Schuyler, James. *Freely Espousing.* New York: Paris Review Editions.

The tonic resonance of / pill when used as in / "she is a pill"

Shapiro, David. *Poems from Deal.* New York: E. P. Dutton.

Did you ever read the wet page of the earth?

Waldman, Anne. *O My Life!.* New York: Angel Hair.

whose impetus is irresistible: / Get out of here!

1970

Ashbery, John. *The Double Dream of Spring.* New York: E.P. Dutton.

They are preparing to begin again: / Problems, new pennant up the flagpole / In a predicated romance.

Ashbery, John. *Evening in the Country.* San Francisco: Spanish Main Press. (broadside)

Now as my questioning but admiring gaze expands to magnificent outposts

Ashbery, John. *The New Spirit.* New York: Adventures in Poetry.

You can feel the wind in the room, the curtains are moving in the draft and a door slowly closes.

Ashbery, John. *Some Trees.* 2nd edition: New York: Corinth Books.

Goodbye, Father! Goodbye, pupils. Goodbye, my master and my dame.

Berrigan, Ted. *In the Early Morning Rain.* London: Cape Goliard Press.

Near Paris, there is a boat. Near this boat live the beautiful Woods.

Berrigan, Ted. *Scorpion, Eagle & Dove.* n.p.: Privately published. (broadside)

where green changes itself into LIFE

Brainard, Joe. *I Remember.* New York: Angel Hair.

I remember jerking off to sexual fantasies involving John Kerr. And Montgomery Clift.

Brodey, Jim. *Zip Guns in the Haunted Mayonnaise.* (not available)

Brownstein, Michael. *3 American Tantrums.* New York: Angel Hair.

But Ned is lazy, the monkey has to do it all.

Carroll, Jim. *4 Ups & 1 Down.* New York: Angel Hair.

like watching wind push seaflowers / straight accross your eyelids

Coolidge, Clark. *Space.* New York: Harper & Row.

file prayer tines

Fagin, Larry. *Brain Damage.* Paris: Sand Project Press.

I stagered from the car nut reall hurt jus shok op

Gallup, Dick. *Where I Hang My Hat.* New York: Harper & Row.

We live in our own hip pocket / nodding out to rush back in.

Gilfillan, Merrill. *Truck.* New York: Angel Hair.

the grin of sleep is in the wind:

Leon [pseud. Larry Fagin, Ron Padgett, Michael Brownstein, Bill Berkson, Lewis Warsh]. *More Pictures of Leon.* New York: Leon Press.

If things are / the way we say they are / then why do we say they are

Mathews, Harry. *The Ring.* Leeds: Juillard Editions.

Have I worn out my distracting powers to doze witless / Into the scape of night, empty of detail and excuse

Padgett, Ron [Jim Dine, illus]. *The Adventures of Mr and Mrs Jim and Ron.* London: Cape Goliard Press/New York: Grossman Publishers.

~~And~~ for the first time in many years Kafka's mother enters the room to kiss him good-night

Towle, Tony. *North.* New York: Columbia University Press / Frank O'Hara Foundation.

I look at the Himalayas; they neither sit nor stand

Veitch, Tom. *Death College.* New York: Siamese Banana Press.

Not the shadow you leave behind / but the opening ahead

Veitch, Tom. *My Father's Golden Eye.* New York: Adventures in Poetry.

Depersonalized angels refer you to nothing and you are nothing / meat stencils

Waldman, Anne. *22.* New York: Handmade book.

It's me (was) & now it's you

Waldman, Anne. *Giant Night.* New York: Corinth Books.

I want to walk around in you breezily, o world, when I'm young.

Process Statement

"Ode: Salute to the New York School" is a cento, a late Roman verse form made up of lines from other sources. First, I put together a chronological bibliography of over 100 books published by New York poets from 1950 to 1970. Many of these books are deeply out of print so I had to do some real digging. Then I extracted lines from each book to compose the cento. Happily, Clark Coolidge supplied lines from the books I couldn't find. The cento also works as an index to the bibliography. The combined bibliography and cento form the libretto to a musical work for the composer Richard Alan Applebaum. My intention was to make what I call a "performing bibliography." Since this is, in effect, what most of us do on a daily basis – referring to or performing what we've read – it seemed a useful metaphor to describe how we enact our reading practice. My idea was that a simple accompaniment to a series of bibliographic entries could generate both scholarly information and an emotive effect. I wanted to express the latent desire for lists and order, and to create a texture to accommodate the eros inherent in research. What I learned along the way is that literary movements survive primarily in the ruins of the texts they leave behind rather than in the unified literary histories that we create for them after the fact.

P.G. 1997

Acknowledgments

This piece was first delivered in March 1996 at the invitation of Stephen Paul Miller & Terence Diggory for their panel on the New York School at The Popular Culture Association Conference, University of Nevada at Las Vegas. The piece subsequently appeared in the following publications: *Chain*, No. 4., Eds. Jena Osman & Juliana Spahr (1997, earlier version); *The Mississippi Review*, Vol. 31, No. 3., Ed. David Lehman (2003, expanded version); and *Against Expression: An Anthology of Conceptual Writing.*, Eds. Craig Dworkin & Kenneth Goldsmith. Evanston: Northwestern UP (2011, cento only). Many thanks to all involved.

PETER GIZZI IS THE AUTHOR OF *Threshold Songs* (Wesleyan, 2011), *The Outernationale* (Wesleyan, 2007), *Some Values of Landscape and Weather* (Wesleyan, 2003), *Artificial Heart* (Burning Deck, 1998), and *Periplum* (Avec Books, 1992). He has also published several limited-edition chapbooks, folios, and artist books and his work has been translated into numerous languages. He is the editor of *The House That Jack Built: The Collected Lectures of Jack Spicer* (Wesleyan, 1998) and, with Kevin Killian, *My Vocabulary Did This To Me: The Collected Poetry of Jack Spicer* (Wesleyan, 2008). In 2011 he was The Judith E. Wilson Visiting Fellow in Poetry at Cambridge University. He works at the University of Massachusetts, Amherst.

Letter Machine Editions

Anselm Berrigan, *To Hell With Sleep*

Edmund Berrigan, *Can It!*

Peter Gizzi, *Ode: Salute to The New York School*

Aaron Kunin, *Grace Period*

Juliana Leslie, *More Radiant Signal*

Farid Matuk, *This Isa Nice Neighborhood*

Sawako Nakayasu, *Texture Notes*

Travis Nichols, *Iowa*

Andrea Rexilius, *Half of What They Carried Flew Away*

Sara Veglahn, *Another Random Heart*

John Yau, *Exhibits*